The Mini-Blender Kitchen

Blender Recipes to Transform Your Day

By: Layla Tacy

Copyright © 2021 by Layla Tacy

License Notes

The content of this publication is protected by national and international copyright laws. Hence, you may not reproduce, edit, copy, print, or distribute any part of it, except with express permission of the author.

The author also reserves the right not to be liable for any inference, assumption, or misinterpretation which might lead to any form of damage.

Table of Contents

Introduction 5

   The Peaches "N" Creamy Blast 7

   The Frozen Mojito 9

   Almond Banana and Fennel Protein Shake 11

   Strawberry with Groundnuts Plus Peach, Mango, and Green Smoothie 13

   The Foundation of Youth Recipe 15

   The Classic Banana Split Smoothie 17

   The Beauty Blast 19

   Strawberry Soup a La Kiev 21

   Sweet Yogurt with Strawberries 23

   The Low-Fat Dragonfly and Banana Milkshake 25

   The Low-Fat Raspberry Banana with Oat Milkshake 27

   The Summer Breeze Smoothie 29

   The Goji Berry Sunrise Smoothie 31

   Avocado Protein Smoothie Recipe 33

   Strawberry Guava with Coconut Shake Recipe 35

The Banana Breakfast Smoothie Recipe 37

Vegan Spiced Pumpkin Chocolate Smoothie 39

The Peachy Keen Banana Smoothie Recipe 41

The Skinny Blast 43

Fresh Fruit with Yoghurt Ice Pops 45

The Sleepy Seeds Recipe 47

The Cholesterol Crusher Blast 49

Matcha Green Tea Smoothie 51

The Tropical Banana-Pineapple Smoothie 53

The Delicious Mango Shakes 55

The Refreshing Watermelon Smoothie 57

Strawberry with Peach Mango and Green Smoothie 59

The Hormone Rejuvenator 61

The Melon-Berry Milkshake 63

The Cabbage Peach with Flax Protein, Smoothie 65

Author's Afterthoughts 67

Biography 68

Introduction

Blenders are one of our favorite kitchen appliances. Small enough for it to be practical and way easier to clean than a conventional blender, there's no reason for us not to love it! It also looks super cute on the counter, which can't hurt either. However, what we most love about it is its blending power!

We love using our Blenders for making smoothies, shakes, sauces, and anything else that we need to blend! Fruits, veggies, nuts, oats, ice, you name it! The thing is, we're not so sure you're reaping all of the benefits you could be getting out of it... that's why we've put together The Mini-Blender Kitchen for you.

With our help, we're going to show you a collection of blended recipes to get your imagination going about everything you can do with a Blender! For example, we've got mojitos, protein shakes, soup, smoothies, ice pops, milkshakes, and so much more. By the look on your face, you haven't been putting your Blender to that good of a use. It's not a once-a-week appliance. Trust us, and it's an everyday one! So, let's get started! Good luck!

xxxxxxxxxxxxxxxxxxxxxxxxxxxxxxxxxxxxxxxxxxxxxxxxxxxxxxx

The Peaches "N" Creamy Blast

This creamy recipe is delicious for the entire family.

Total Prep Time: 5 minutes

Serving Sizes: 1-2

List of Ingredients:

- ½ a cup of plain yogurt
- ½ a cup of frozen peaches
- ½ a large banana
- 1 tbsp. of sesame seeds
- 1 cup of vanilla coconut (unsweetened) or almond milk
- 3 ice cubes

xxxxxxxxxxxxxxxxxxxxxxxxxxxxxxxxxxxxxxxxxxxxxxxxxxxxx

Methods:

Add all the ingredients into the Blender then extract for about 45 seconds and consume immediately.

The Frozen Mojito

This is one of the coolest and one of the most refreshing drinks you can ever ask for. It is packed with some of the finest natural ingredients.

Total Prep Time: 5 minutes

Serving Sizes: 1-2

List of Ingredients:

- ½ of a cup of fresh mint
- 1 peeled and sectioned lime
- 1 large frozen banana
- 1 cup of fresh spinach
- 3 small ice cubes
- 1 dash of honey or agave (optional)

xxxxxxxxxxxxxxxxxxxxxxxxxxxxxxxxxxxxxxxxxxxxxxxxxxxx

Methods:

Add all the ingredients to the large cup of the Blender, and extract for about 1 minute until the blend is perfectly smooth. You can add a dash of rum to it before serving.

Almond Banana and Fennel Protein Shake

This smoothie is rich in protein, can help you create lean muscles, and support speedy fat loss.

Total Prep Time: 5 minutes

Serving Sizes: 1

List of Ingredients:

- ½ of a cup almond milk
- ½ of a medium of sliced banana
- ½ of a cup of shredded fennel bulb
- 1 scoop of soy protein powder

xxxxxxxxxxxxxxxxxxxxxxxxxxxxxxxxxxxxxxxxxxxxxxxxxxx

Methods:

Combine the entire ingredients inside the long glass container on the Blender and blend perfectly for about 45 seconds to extract the juice. Serve cold or refrigerate.

Strawberry with Groundnuts Plus Peach, Mango, and Green Smoothie

Adding nuts to this smoothie will make the drink more nutritious, especially for the protein and omega 3 fatty acids.

Total Prep Time: 10 minutes

Serving Sizes: 1-2

List of Ingredients:

- ¼ of cup of groundnut (or any other alternative nut)
- ¾ of a cup of rainbow chard
- ½ of medium pomegranate (scoop the inside with the pith remaining intact)
- 1/2 a cup of a mix of different berries (blueberries, raspberries, and blackberries)
- ½ a cup of unsweetened coconut milk

xxxxxxxxxxxxxxxxxxxxxxxxxxxxxxxxxxxxxxxxxxxxxxxxxxxx

Methods:

Add everything into the Blender and blend properly until the mix is smooth. Serve immediate.

The Foundation of Youth Recipe

Appear and feel refreshed and better than you were a few years ago with this natural Blender recipe.

Total Prep Time: 5 minutes

Serving Sizes: 1-2

List of Ingredients:

- ½ of a large avocado (pitted and peeled)
- 2 handfuls of Kale
- 1 medium size of a pitted medium nectarine
- ½ a cup of blueberries
- 10 walnut halves

xxxxxxxxxxxxxxxxxxxxxxxxxxxxxxxxxxxxxxxxxxxxxxxxxxxx

Methods:

Fill the Blender to the maximum line and add some almond milk or water before extracting for about 2 minutes. Serve immediately or refrigerate.

The Classic Banana Split Smoothie

The classic banana split smoothie is all you need this summer season. It is so refreshing and amazing.

Serving Sizes: 2-3

Total Prep Time: 25 minutes

List of Ingredients:

- 2 whole medium-size ripe fresh or frozen Chiquita banana
- 2 cups of ice
- ½ cup non-fat vanilla yogurt
- 2 crushed nuts
- 6 maraschino cherries

xxxxxxxxxxxxxxxxxxxxxxxxxxxxxxxxxxxxxxxxxxxxxxxxx

Methods:

Add the Chiquita bananas with the yogurt and cherries in a Blender before adding the crushed nuts and ice. Blend the mixture for about 90 seconds until it becomes smooth.

The addition of ice will help create a good blend; however, you must ensure that the ice does not soften the smoothie excessively. This smoothie will provide a serving that will last a few days or a week. Serve immediately.

The Beauty Blast

If you are ready to reclaim your youthful glow, then you should consider this wonderful Blender recipe.

Total Prep Time: 4 minutes

Serving Sizes: 1-2

List of Ingredients:

- 2 handful of Swiss Chard
- ½ of a cup of pineapple
- ½ a cup of strawberries
- 1 tbsp. of goji berries
- 12 medium to large cashews

xxxxxxxxxxxxxxxxxxxxxxxxxxxxxxxxxxxxxxxxxxxxxxxxxxxxxxx

Methods:

Fill the Blender to the maximum limit, add some water, and extract for few minutes before serving.

Strawberry Soup a La Kiev

Total Prep Time: 10 minutes

Serving Sizes: 8

List of Ingredients:

- 3-4 cups of strawberries (chopped)
- A cup of brown sugar
- A cup of sour cream
- 4 cups of fresh cold water
- A cup of your favorite red wine (preferably Burgundy)

xxxxxxxxxxxxxxxxxxxxxxxxxxxxxxxxxxxxxxxxxxxxxxxxxxxxx

Methods:

Puree the strawberry inside a Blender and pour it inside a large saucepan. (10 minutes)

Stir in the brown sugar, sour cream, wine, and water. Cook it over low to medium heat, and stir gently for about 20 minutes to ensure the flavors are thoroughly blended in. Do not allow the soup to boil. Just serve it warm. (20 minutes).

Sweet Yogurt with Strawberries

Yogurt with strawberries is a nutritional boost to the body any day.

Total Prep Time: 10 minutes

Serving Sizes: 1-2

List of Ingredients:

- A cup of fresh quartered strawberries
- A tsp. of brown sugar
- A cup of fat-free yogurt (plain or strawberry)
- ¼ cup slivered toasted almonds
- ¼ cup low-fat granola

xxxxxxxxxxxxxxxxxxxxxxxxxxxxxxxxxxxxxxxxxxxxxxxxxxx

Methods:

Toss the cup of strawberries with brown sugar and then add unto the middle of a cereal bowl holding the fat-free yogurt, blend in the Blender. Top up with the toasted almonds and low-fat granola and serve immediately.

The Low-Fat Dragonfly and Banana Milkshake

This is a mild smoothie that can energize your body, especially after performing an intense workout session.

Total Prep Time: 10 minutes

Serving Sizes: 1-2

List of Ingredients:

- ½ of a medium, sliced dragon fruit
- ½ of a medium, sliced banana
- ½ of a cup of low-fat milk
- ¼ of a cup of crushed ice

xxxxxxxxxxxxxxxxxxxxxxxxxxxxxxxxxxxxxxxxxxxxxxxxxxxx

Methods:

Combine all the ingredients inside the tall glass of the Blender, then blend perfectly for about 45 seconds. Pour inside a glass or 2 glasses and garnish with a little slice of dragon fruit (optional). Serve immediately.

The Low-Fat Raspberry Banana with Oat Milkshake

This is a nutritious recipe with lots of antioxidants, vitamins, and minerals.

Total Prep Time: 10 minutes

Serving Sizes: 1

List of Ingredients:

- ½ a cup of frozen raspberries
- ½ a medium-size frozen banana
- 1 tbsp. of rolled oats
- ½ a cup of low-fat milk
- ¼ of a cup of crushed ice

xxxxxxxxxxxxxxxxxxxxxxxxxxxxxxxxxxxxxxxxxxxxxxxxxxxxxxx

Methods:

Combine all the ingredients inside the tall glass of the Blender and blend for about a minute until the mix is smooth. Pour inside a glass and garnish with a slice of banana if you desire.

Serve immediately or refrigerate.

The Summer Breeze Smoothie

Total Prep Time: 5 minutes

Serving Sizes: 3

List of Ingredients:

- A cup of plain non-fat yogurt
- 6 medium to large strawberries
- A cup of crushed pineapple
- 1 medium or large banana
- A tsp. of vanilla extract
- 4 ice cubes

xxxxxxxxxxxxxxxxxxxxxxxxxxxxxxxxxxxxxxxxxxxxxxxxxxxxx

Methods:

Place all the ingredients in a Blender and extract until perfectly smooth serve immediately in frosted glass.

The Goji Berry Sunrise Smoothie

Goji berries are delicious and packed with phytonutrients, including antioxidants.

Serving Sizes: 8

Total Prep Time: 30 minutes or less

List of Ingredients:

- Two, 10 to 15 oz. cans of light coconut milk
- Two 1 ½ cups of frozen fresh pineapple chunks
- ¾ cup of fresh frozen mango cubes
- ¼ cup of unflavored pea-protein powder
- ¼ cup of Goji berries
- 1 tbsp. of agave nectar

xxxxxxxxxxxxxxxxxxxxxxxxxxxxxxxxxxxxxxxxxxxxxxxxxxxx

Methods:

Blend all these ingredients in the Blender until perfectly smooth. Serve immediately or store in the refrigerator.

Avocado Protein Smoothie Recipe

Avocado is a miracle food rich in Omega 3 and 6, and this recipe will surely make your day.

Total Prep Time: 7 minutes

Serving Sizes: 1-2

List of Ingredients:

- 1 small peeled and pitted ripe avocado
- 1 cup of coconut milk
- ½ a cup of coconut water
- 2 tbsp. of honey
- ½ a cup of mango cubes

xxxxxxxxxxxxxxxxxxxxxxxxxxxxxxxxxxxxxxxxxxxxxxxxxxxxxxxx

Methods:

Place all the ingredients inside the Blender processor, and blend very well. Serve immediately or with some dash of ice cubes.

Strawberry Guava with Coconut Shake Recipe

Not everyone likes guava, but this recipe will surely give you a nutritional boost for those courageous enough to enjoy the taste.

Total Prep Time: 10 minutes

Serving Sizes: 1-2

List of Ingredients:

- 3 cups of halved strawberries
- 1 medium sliced guava
- 3-5 crushed ice cubes
- ¼ cup of coconut water

xxxxxxxxxxxxxxxxxxxxxxxxxxxxxxxxxxxxxxxxxxxxxxxxxxxxxx

Methods:

Place the ingredients inside a tall glass in the Blender, blend properly until the mix is well-blended, pour inside the glass, and add the ice before serving.

The Banana Breakfast Smoothie Recipe

Banana is ideal for detox. Hence this smoothie can rejuvenate your digestive system.

Serving Sizes: 2-3

Total Prep Time: 30 minutes

List of Ingredients:

- ½ a cup of 1% low fat skimmed milk
- ½ a cup of crushed ice
- a tbsp. of honey
- 1/8 spoon of crushed nutmeg
- 2 slice ripe and frozen large bananas
- 1 cup of 2% plain Greek yogurt

xxxxxxxxxxxxxxxxxxxxxxxxxxxxxxxxxxxxxxxxxxxxxxxxxxxxxx

Methods:

Combine all the ingredients in the blender, and blend for a couple of minutes until perfectly smooth. You can add the plain yogurt before or after blending and serve the smoothie immediately.

Vegan Spiced Pumpkin Chocolate Smoothie

If you desire some special sugar-free Halloween recipe this season, you should consider this Blender recipe.

Total Prep Time: 10 minutes

Serving Sizes: 1-2

List of Ingredients:

- ¾ of a cup of full-fat coconut milk
- 1 tbsp. of vanilla protein powder (optional)
- 1 tbsp. of almond butter
- ½ of a tsp. of ground cinnamon
- ½ of a tsp. of ground ginger
- ¼ of a tsp. of nutmeg
- ½ a tsp. of raw cacao powder
- ½ a cup of pumpkin puree
- ¼ spoon of salt

xxxxxxxxxxxxxxxxxxxxxxxxxxxxxxxxxxxxxxxxxxxxxxxxxxxxx

Methods:

Add all ingredients into a blender and blend very well for about 2 minutes, then pour it into a glass cup and serve with ice (optional). You can freeze or refrigerate the drink also.

The Peachy Keen Banana Smoothie Recipe

Ripe and juicy peaches can work perfectly well with bananas to provide an excellent, tasty, and healthy detox smoothie for weight loss. It would help if you kept in mind that Chiquita bananas must make up 70% of this recipe.

Total Prep Time: 10 minutes

Serving Sizes: 2-3

List of Ingredients:

- 2 whole Chiquita bananas (these must be peeled, chopped or sliced and frozen)
- 1 cup of peach
- 1 cup of non-fat Greek vanilla yogurt.

xxxxxxxxxxxxxxxxxxxxxxxxxxxxxxxxxxxxxxxxxxxxxxxxxxx

Methods:

Place all the ingredients in a clean Blender and make sure they do not fill more than 2/3rd length of the mixer, puree the mix until it smoothens to your desired texture.

You can also make this smoothie with unfrozen Chiquita bananas. However, you may not get the kind of thick texture you would with frozen bananas. You can also garnish this smoothie with some slices of banana and peaches.

The Skinny Blast

Are you looking to shed some extra weight? This recipe may offer much-needed assistance.

Total Prep Time: 5 minutes

Serving Sizes: 1-2

List of Ingredients:

- 1 large banana
- 2 hand-full of chopped spinach
- 1/8 of a cup of pumpkin seeds
- 1 peeled orange
- 1 large carrot
- 2 tbsp. of hemp seed

xxxxxxxxxxxxxxxxxxxxxxxxxxxxxxxxxxxxxxxxxxxxxxxxxxxxxx

Methods:

Fill the Blender to the maximum limit, then add some almond milk or water and extract immediately. Serve immediately or chill in the refrigerator.

Fresh Fruit with Yoghurt Ice Pops

Yoghurt pops will make your day so refreshing.

Total Prep Time: 50 minutes

Serving Sizes: 8

List of Ingredients:

- 2 cups of a mix of strawberries, raspberries, blueberries, and diced bananas
- 2 cups of vanilla or plain yogurt
- ¼ cup of brown sugar
- 8 popsicle sticks
- 8 small paper cups

xxxxxxxxxxxxxxxxxxxxxxxxxxxxxxxxxxxxxxxxxxxxxxxxxxx

Methods:

Place all the fruits and the yogurt in a Blender, then cover and blend until the mix becomes smooth or chunky, as desired. (4 minutes)

Fill up the paper cups 3/ 4 full of the fruit mix, and cover each with a strip of aluminum foil. (2 minutes)

Pop in a Popsicle stick, each at the center of the aluminum foil. You can freeze the cups and their contents for about 40 minutes and remove the aluminum foils when serving. (41 minutes).

The Sleepy Seeds Recipe

This is a flavorful blast that will get your life back on track

Total Prep Time: 5 minutes

Serving Sizes: 1-2

List of Ingredients:

- 2 handfuls of chopped spinach
- 1 large banana
- ¼ of a cup of raspberries
- ¼ of a cup of blueberry
- 1 tbsp. of pumpkin seeds
- 1 tbsp. of sunflower seeds

xxxxxxxxxxxxxxxxxxxxxxxxxxxxxxxxxxxxxxxxxxxxxxxxxxxxx

Methods:

Fill the Blender to the maximum line and add some clean water before extracting for about 2 minutes. Refrigerate or serve immediately.

The Cholesterol Crusher Blast

This is the perfect way of reducing cholesterol naturally.

Total Prep Time: 5 minutes

Serving Sizes: 1-2

List of Ingredients:

- 1 cup of blueberries
- 2 handfuls of kale
- ½ a large banana
- 1/3 of a cup of cooked oatmeal
- 10 large almonds
- 2 tbsp. of raw cacao

xxxxxxxxxxxxxxxxxxxxxxxxxxxxxxxxxxxxxxxxxxxxxxxxxxxx

Methods:

Fill the Blender top to the maximum line with clean water and extract for about 2 minutes. Serve immediately.

Matcha Green Tea Smoothie

Green smoothie helps you detox your vital organs anytime.

Serving Sizes: 6-10

Total Prep Time: 20 minutes

List of Ingredients:

- 2-3 cups of baby spinach
- about 2 cups of rice milk
- a medium peeled and cut avocado
- ½ cup of green grapes
- 2 tbsp. of Matcha green tea
- 2 tbsp. of grated fresh ginger
- Optional 1 tbsp. of agave nectar

xxxxxxxxxxxxxxxxxxxxxxxxxxxxxxxxxxxxxxxxxxxxxxxxxxxxx

Methods:

Blend all the ingredients inside the blender and blend until perfectly smooth.

The Tropical Banana-Pineapple Smoothie

Total Prep Time: 30 minutes

Serving Sizes: 2 cups

List of Ingredients:

- 2 large Chiquita bananas or 2 cups of peeled,
- sliced and frozen banana,
- ½ cup of skimmed non-fat milk, and
- 3 oz. of chopped Pineapple or juice.

xxxxxxxxxxxxxxxxxxxxxxxxxxxxxxxxxxxxxxxxxxxxxxxxxxxxxx

Methods:

Pour the ingredients into a blender and blend for about 40 seconds until the smoothie becomes thick. You may add an optional 1 tbsp. of almond to this smoothie.

The Delicious Mango Shakes

Mango is good for the skin, and you will love this recipe.

Total Prep Time: 7 minutes

Serving Sizes: 4

List of Ingredients:

- 2 cups of milk (1-5% fat)
- 8 tbsp. of fresh mango juice, or 1 pitted mango
- 1 large banana
- 2 ice cubes

xxxxxxxxxxxxxxxxxxxxxxxxxxxxxxxxxxxxxxxxxxxxxxxxxxxx

Methods:

Add all ingredients in the Blender, then blend until it becomes foamy and serve immediately fresh.

The Refreshing Watermelon Smoothie

Watermelon comes with very low calories, and it is packed with amino acids- citrulline and arginine, which are known to provide smooth blood flow and make the heart-healthy.

Total Prep Time: 10 minutes

Serving Sizes: 1

List of Ingredients:

- 1 ½ cup of sliced watermelon
- ½ a cup of strawberries
- 1/3 of a cup of beets
- ¼ of a cup of diced coconut

xxxxxxxxxxxxxxxxxxxxxxxxxxxxxxxxxxxxxxxxxxxxxxxxxxxxx

Methods:

Fill up the Blender till maximum line and add some coconut water before blending perfectly for few minutes. Serve immediately or refrigerate.

Strawberry with Peach Mango and Green Smoothie

The recipe is loaded with vitamin c and can also be the ideal workout smoothie for those early mornings.

Total Prep Time: 10 minutes

Serving Sizes: 1-2

List of Ingredients:

- 1 cup of rainbow chard
- ½ of medium pomegranate (scoop the inside with the pith remaining intact)
- 1/2 a cup of a mix of different berries (blueberries, raspberries, and blackberries)
- ½ a cup of unsweetened coconut milk

xxxxxxxxxxxxxxxxxxxxxxxxxxxxxxxxxxxxxxxxxxxxxxxxxxxxx

Methods:

Add everything into the Blender and blend properly until the mix is smooth. Serve immediate.

The Hormone Rejuvenator

Hormonal changes are inevitable, but you don't have to suffer, especially when consuming the right food ingredients.

Total Prep Time: 5 minutes

Serving Sizes: 1-2

List of Ingredients:

- ¼ of small raw beets
- 10 seedless red grapes
- 2 small broccoli florets
- 10 raspberries
- 1 tbsp. of goji berries
- ½ of a small to medium avocado (peeled and pitted)
- 1 tsp. of olive oil.

xxxxxxxxxxxxxxxxxxxxxxxxxxxxxxxxxxxxxxxxxxxxxxxxxxxxxxxx

Methods:

Fill the Blender to its maximum line with some coconut oil and extract for about 2 minutes.

Serve immediately and enjoy.

The Melon-Berry Milkshake

A great home-made milkshake you will relish always

Total Prep Time: 10 minutes

Serving Sizes: 1-2

List of Ingredients:

- 2 wedges of cut cantaloupe
- 1 cup of fresh or frozen blueberries
- 1 tbsp. of chia seeds
- ½ a cup of unsweetened almond milk (plain)

xxxxxxxxxxxxxxxxxxxxxxxxxxxxxxxxxxxxxxxxxxxxxxxxxxxxx

Methods:

Add everything inside the Blender and blend perfectly for about 2 minutes until smooth.

Serve immediately or refrigerate.

The Cabbage Peach with Flax Protein, Smoothie

This is a protein-rich smoothie with lots of nutrients that will transform your body.

Total Prep Time: 10 minutes

Serving Sizes: 1-2

List of Ingredients:

- ½ cup of shredded cabbage
- 1 medium sliced peach
- 1 scoop of vanilla whey protein powder
- 1 tsp. of flaxseed
- ½ a cup of water

xxxxxxxxxxxxxxxxxxxxxxxxxxxxxxxxxxxxxxxxxxxxxxxxxxxx

Methods:

Combine all the ingredients inside the tall glass in the Blender and blend perfectly for about 1 minute, then pour inside a glass and serve immediately or chill in the refrigerator.

Author's Afterthoughts

I can't appreciate you enough for spending your precious time reading my book. If there is anything that gladdens an author's heart, it is that his or her work be read. And I am extremely joyous that my labor and the hours put into making this publication a reality didn't go to waste.

Another thing that gladdens an author's heart is feedback because every comment from the good people who read one's book matters a great deal in helping you become better at what you do.

This is why I wouldn't shy away from reading your thoughts and comments about what you have read in this publication.

Do you think it is good enough? Do you think it could be better?

Please keep the feedback coming in, I won't hesitate to read any of them!!!

Thanks!

Layla Tacy

Biography

Climbing up the ladder from a young girl who loved to experiment with food items in her mother's cottage kitchen at the tender age of 7, to changing cooking from what it was to what it should be; Layla has more than made a name for herself, but she has created a dynasty for herself in the cooking world.

With more than twenty-five years in the culinary world, Layla has grown to be an authority with her influence spreading all over different high-class hotels and restaurants in and around Kansas City, such as Hilton President Kansas City, The Fountaine hotel, and Embassy Suites.

After working as a chef in different establishments, Layla moved on to become a chef-trainer to several up-and-coming chefs. Currently, she has graduated more than 200 trainees at her Chef School and presently has about 150 graduates in her school.

Made in the USA
Las Vegas, NV
06 April 2025